You Wouldn't Want to Meet Burke and Hare!

This body is mingin!
(This body smells awful!)

Written by
Fiona Macdonald

Illustrated by
David Antram

Body Snatchers You'd Rather Avoid

Created and designed by
David Salariya

BOOK HOUSE
a SALARIYA *imprint*

Contents

Author:

Fiona Macdonald studied history at
Cambridge University and at the University of
East Anglia. She has taught in adult education,
schools and colleges, and is the author of
numerous books for children on historical topics.

Artist:

David Antram was born in Brighton, England,
in 1958. He studied at Eastbourne College of
Art and then worked in advertising for fifteen
years before becoming a full-time artist. He has
illustrated many children's nonfiction books.

Series Creator:

David Salariya was born in Dundee, Scotland.
He has illustrated a wide range of books and has
created and designed many new series for
publishers both in the U.K. and overseas. In 1989,
he established The Salariya Book Company. He
lives in Brighton, England, with his wife, illustrator
Shirley Willis, and their son Jonathan.

Published in Great Britain in MMXXI by
Book House, an imprint of
The Salariya Book Company Ltd
25 Marlborough Place, Brighton BN1 1UB
www.salariya.com

ISBN: 978-1-913337-68-1

SCRIBO BOOK HOUSE SCRIBBLERS

1 3 5 7 9 8 6 4 2

A CIP catalogue record for this book is available
from the British Library.
Printed and bound in China.

Visit
www.salariya.com
for our online catalogue and
free fun stuff.

PAPER FROM
SUSTAINABLE
FORESTS

Introduction

Edinburgh, Scotland, 1828

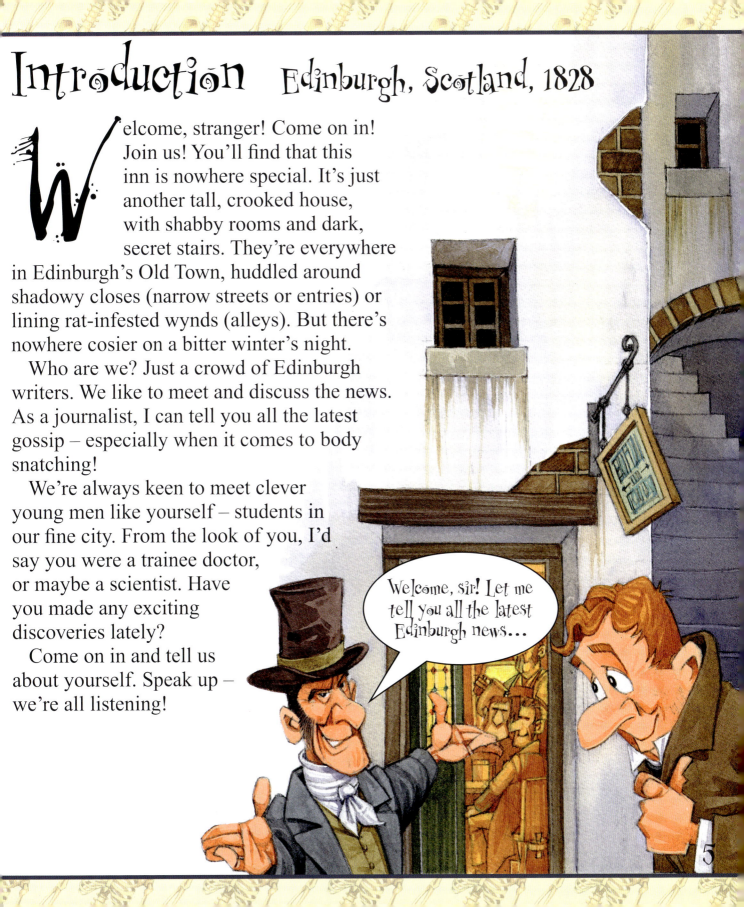

Welcome, stranger! Come on in! Join us! You'll find that this inn is nowhere special. It's just another tall, crooked house, with shabby rooms and dark, secret stairs. They're everywhere in Edinburgh's Old Town, huddled around shadowy closes (narrow streets or entries) or lining rat-infested wynds (alleys). But there's nowhere cosier on a bitter winter's night.

Who are we? Just a crowd of Edinburgh writers. We like to meet and discuss the news. As a journalist, I can tell you all the latest gossip – especially when it comes to body snatching!

We're always keen to meet clever young men like yourself – students in our fine city. From the look of you, I'd say you were a trainee doctor, or maybe a scientist. Have you made any exciting discoveries lately?

Come on in and tell us about yourself. Speak up – we're all listening!

Welcome, sir! Let me tell you all the latest Edinburgh news...

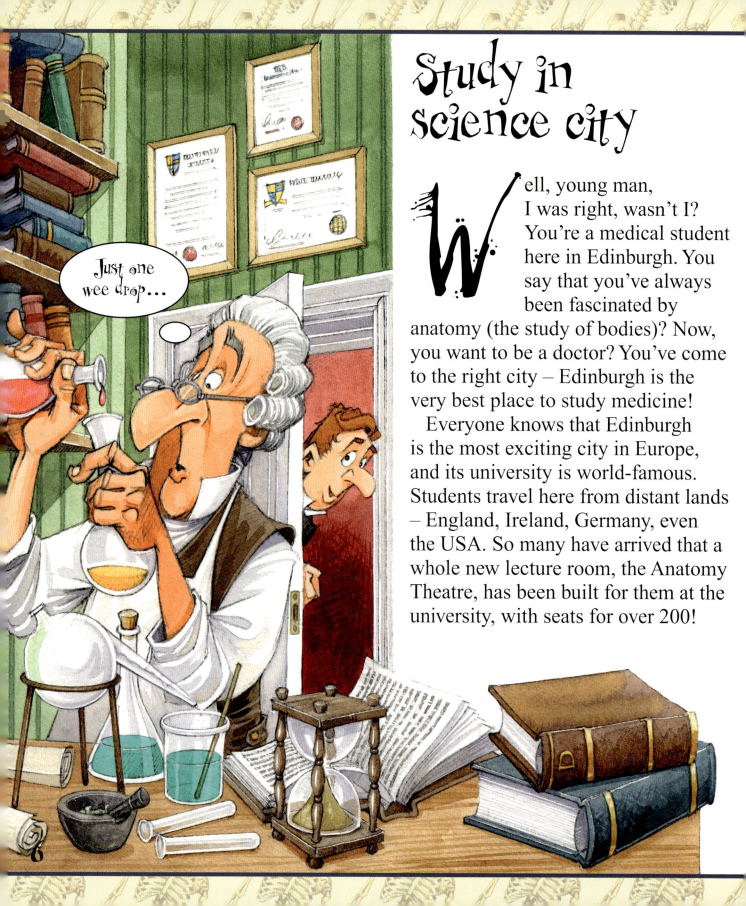

Just one wee drop...

Study in science city

Well, young man, I was right, wasn't I? You're a medical student here in Edinburgh. You say that you've always been fascinated by anatomy (the study of bodies)? Now, you want to be a doctor? You've come to the right city – Edinburgh is the very best place to study medicine!

Everyone knows that Edinburgh is the most exciting city in Europe, and its university is world-famous. Students travel here from distant lands – England, Ireland, Germany, even the USA. So many have arrived that a whole new lecture room, the Anatomy Theatre, has been built for them at the university, with seats for over 200!

Old slums

OLD. Edinburgh's Old Town is Scotland's ancient capital. There are streets lined with tall, shabby houses. But there's also the magnificent Edinburgh castle, a royal palace, and a Botanic Garden full of medicinal plants. The Old Town is so full of history!

Surgeon's Square

Handy hint

If you want to learn, join a club! How about Edinburgh's famous Poker Club? Its members 'stir up' new ideas, just as a poker stirs up a fire.

NEW. Edinburgh's New Town is the modern quarter of the city, built during the past 50 years. The University is here, and the Teaching Hospital, as well as libraries, museums and Surgeon's Square.

Robert Burns, poet

Adam Smith, philosopher

James Watt, inventor

David Hume, philosopher

Robert Adam, architect

GREAT MINDS. There's a famous saying about Edinburgh: 'If you stand in the main street for an afternoon, you'll be able to shake 50 men of genius by the hand.'

That sounds very boastful, but it's not far from the truth. Writers, thinkers, doctors, scientists, engineers – they've all taught or studied here! Their achievements are famous worldwide.

The good doctor

Young man, I must ask you: have you met Dr Knox? He's one of Britain's leading scientists. Famous and fashionable, he lives here in Edinburgh. They say he's a brilliant teacher, who makes medicine fun. He has over 500 students. To teach them all, he has to repeat each lecture three times!

Have you been to any of his demonstrations, where he dissects (cuts up) dead bodies and explains them? What's that? Knox is your hero? You want to investigate bodies, just like him, and save lots of lives!

Observe the subject's heart, a vital organ that pumps blood around the body...

A brilliant career

AT SCHOOL, he wins a medal for being 'dux' (a Latin word for 'leader' or 'best student').

THE YEAR after graduating, he gets great praise for a scientific paper.

KNOX JOINS the army. In 1815 he cares for soldiers injured at the epic Battle of Waterloo.

ROBERT KNOX: Born 1791. He gets smallpox and loses an eye, but this doesn't stop him learning.

AT EDINBURGH university, he works hard to become a doctor, but also finds time for parties.

KNOX GOES to Paris, France, and studies with Georges Cuvier, the world's best anatomist (a scientist who studies bodies).

That's so interesting!

Look at that waistcoat!

Look at that blood!

Handy hint

Keep counting! As a student in Edinburgh, you'll have to cut up three bodies before you can qualify as a doctor.

Silhouette of Dr Knox

LOOKING GOOD. Friends describe Knox as a strong, well-built person. He loves to wear expensive, fashionable clothes – even while giving lectures and cutting up dead bodies!

ANATOMY AND Physiology.

Notice advertising Dr Knox's lectures, 1828

RETURNING to Edinburgh, Knox becomes a Fellow of the Royal Society of Edinburgh – a top scientific honour.

KNOX TAKES charge of – and adds to – the famous collection of preserved body parts at Surgeon's Square, Edinburgh.

IN 1826, KNOX becomes head of the anatomy school in Edinburgh.

DEAD WRONG. Clever though he was, we now know that Dr Knox had ideas about race that were completely mistaken.

More modern medicine

Traditionally, medicine has been divided between doctors (or 'physicians') and barber-surgeons. Barber-surgeons stitched cuts and amputated limbs. They were craftsmen, rather than educated professionals. Physicians mostly treated people with medicines. But times have changed, and now – thanks to the medical schools in Edinburgh and other European cities – there's a growing group of trained medical doctors who can perform surgery.

Eyeballs in a jar? Oh, how deliciously ghastly!

Educated surgeons include Scottish brothers William and John Hunter, who became famous in London. When John died in 1793, he left an amazing collection of 10,563 body-part specimens! In London, there are also public exhibitions of specimens preserved in glass jars. They are educational, but also make money as vulgar entertainment.

Handy hint

Keep your specimens safe! William Hunter built a new house with a room for dissecting bodies and a private museum!

What am I removing, again?

This might hurt…

PROGRESS.
In the past 50 years, the scientific study of bodies has helped to improve many medical treatments, such as pulling rotten teeth.

A CUT ABOVE.
Surgeons have learned how to cut bullets out of muscles and stitch up gunshot wounds.

SCIENTISTS like Edward Jenner (1749–1823) have experimented with new techniques of fighting killer diseases, such as vaccination against smallpox.

SURGEON William Hunter (1718–1783) became an expert on childbirth. He was made physician to Queen Charlotte, and professor of anatomy at the Royal Academy of Arts.

11

All for art

ANIMAL ART. Rich families like portraits of their favourite hunting or race-horses. Some animal artists have to dissect huge creatures for study.

There is another group of people who investigate bodies – painters and sculptors. I find out a lot from visiting their studios, along with my fellow journalists. Today's artists like to create realistic portraits, heroic scenes from myths, or action-packed battle pictures. Many artists pay living models to pose for them.

BEASTLY. Farmers today are breeding new, bigger animals, and they want portraits of them. But you'll have to paint these prize beasts alive!

NEED FOR SPEED. If you're using dead bodies as models, you have to paint very quickly. They rot – and smell dreadful – after just a few days.

DISPOSAL. Once you've finished with the dead body, you have to get rid of it – without attracting attention.

Can you raise the body's arm up a little?

But some painters feel they need to go a step further in understanding the human body before they can create convincing images. So they have dead bodies discreetly delivered to their studios. They cut them up to study the bones and muscles under the skin, hoping to make their pictures more lifelike.

Handy hint

Travel abroad! See the famous waxworks museum in Florence, Italy. It has 19 life-sized model human bodies to study. They say that the artists had to study 200 real corpses to make each one of them!

The things I do for a living…

Don't do that!

What's that you say? You want to get a body to examine? Oh no! Take my advice – don't do that!

Why? Because most bodies supplied to doctors, scientists and artists have been stolen from graves! According to the law, only dead criminals' bodies can be dissected – and there are not enough of them to go round. Fewer than 100 men and women were hanged in Britain last year, but doctors demanded ten times as many.

There are criminals – professional body snatchers or 'resurrectionists' – who dig up corpses from cemeteries. But they're vicious and violent! Do you really want to meet them?

Moving a snatched body

Cram it into a sack or basket.

Bundle it inside a box or barrel.

Stuff it under straw in a cart.

Tie it up and label it, like a parcel.

Other ways to snatch a body

STEAL IT in broad daylight, from an isolated churchyard.

TAKE THE RECENTLY deceased from the house of a grieving family.

Rest in peace?

No-one wants their dead loved ones dug up for dissection. Many people fear that the dead whose graves are unlawfully disturbed will never rest in peace. They also worry about what might happen to their own bodies after they die. For them, the thought of being body-snatched is almost worse than death itself. A body robbed from a grave has no name, no past and no future.

Body snatching is distressing, offensive and against the law. So families and communities do all they can to stop this loathsome crime!

PAY OUT. Pay for a thick lead casket that's too heavy for body snatchers to carry away.

Wee Aunt Mabel was heavier than she looked!

Security systems

KEEP WATCH. Build towers in burial grounds, so that lookouts can watch for thieves.

LOCK UP. Fit iron straps and locks around wooden coffins. That will keep the lid securely closed.

FENCE IN. Surround churchyards and cemeteries with high walls and spiked metal gates.

LOCK IN. Fix strong iron bars or cages around individual graves or family plots.

BLOCK OUT. Huge stone slabs will make it hard for body snatchers to dig into a grave.

HIRE HELP. Pay tough security guards to patrol and protect graveyards every night.

DIG DEEP. Ask for your loved ones to be buried extra-deep. If snatchers dig too far down, the grave sides will cave in and bury them.

Handy hint

Guard a new grave! Flowers or wreaths will show snatchers where a fresh body has been buried — and will hide traces of grave-robbers.

KEEP CLEAR of body snatchers! They could spread lethal germs and diseases that can be caught from a decaying body.

Filthy rich

Being a body snatcher is difficult and dangerous – so why do people do it? Because body snatchers make an awful lot of money! In just one night of grimy grave-robbing, a body snatcher can earn almost as much as an honest farm worker gets in a year.

Doctors charge high fees to patients and students, so they can afford to pay for bodies. Most medical men don't want to break the law, but a few get carried away by their passion for science, their rivalry with other researchers, or their love of fame. They grow so keen on dissecting that they don't stop to ask – and don't want to know – where the dead bodies come from.

DIRTY DEALS. Dealing with body snatchers will make you a criminal. Your medical career will be over before it has even started – and your life will be in danger from mob attacks.

PUBLIC OUTCRY. Doctors and students in Glasgow, Scotland's second city, have been attacked by the outraged families of victims of body snatchers. Now they have to be guarded by soldiers!

Smash!!!

What a bunch of rats!

It's dead easy to make money in this business.

Handy hint

Don't be deceived! To avoid suspicion, most body snatchers hide their criminal earnings and pretend to be poor.

I'll give you fifteen!

I'll give you ten pounds!

Money troubles

Body snatching is profitable, but snatchers don't get to keep all the money:

TWO'S COMPANY. Body snatchers have to share the cash with their partners – or else they might also end up as dead bodies!

PAY-OFF. They have to pay bribes to curious people who ask awkward questions.

RISKY. They are in constant danger of blackmail from anyone who suspects them or might betray them.

HIGH DEMAND. Prices for bodies are rising. It's the law of supply and demand. As medicine, science and art become more popular and respectable, there are not enough legally supplied dead bodies to go around.

19

A steady supply

William and Margaret Hare

No-one knows how many people die each week in our great city. And, if the deceased were very old or very ill, their remains often prove to be unsuitable for dissection. Because of this, body snatchers are always looking for new places to find corpses. Right now, in 1828, it's rumoured that they are starting to organise a steady supply of bodies – by killing people to order!

I suppose murder is quicker and less risky than digging up graveyards. I've heard that two suspected murderers have just been arrested. Their names are – let me look at my notebook – William Burke and William Hare. Both have sold bodies to your hero, Dr Knox!

William and Helen Burke

SHADY PASTS. Rumour has it that Burke's first wife and children mysteriously disappeared. Hare is suspected of murdering his landlord. Now they share a house in Edinburgh with their new partners and take in lodgers.

IRELAND TO EDINBURGH. William Burke (born 1792) and William Hare (born 1790) are both Irish labourers. Like many other poor people, they have come to Scotland to find work. They've done all kinds of odd jobs, but don't seem to have earned much money.

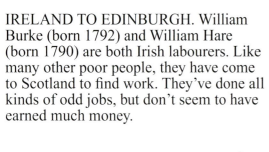

EDINBURGH

No evidence?

’ve heard that Burke and Hare found a way of killing that left no marks on their victims. So, even if a dissected body was traced back to them, no-one could prove that it was murder.

So how did they get caught? It seems that two lodgers in Burke and Hare's house, James and Ann Gray, alerted the police to the duo's shady actions. Another lodger heard strange shouts one night; the next day, Burke was acting suspiciously. So the Grays searched the house and found a body under a bed! Now both men have been arrested.

Ouch!

SECRET SIGNAL. In the crowded lodging house, Helen Burke and Margaret Hare could not say out loud that they had found a new victim to kill. So they gave a secret signal: they stood close to Burke and Hare and, under the cover of their long skirts, gently trod on their husbands' toes.

Typical tactics

HELEN BURKE and Margaret Hare help the murderers by finding and befriending victims.

THEY FIND a likely victim in the Edinburgh streets and invite them into their house to sit and rest by the fire.

THEY FETCH Burke or Hare, and introduce the victim.

Nobody's going to miss this one…

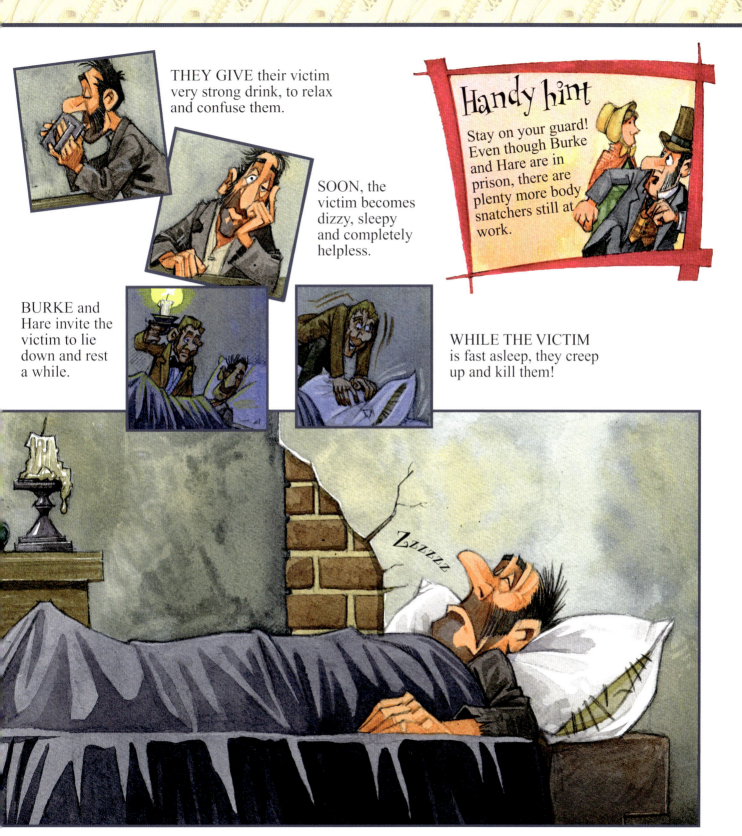

THEY GIVE their victim very strong drink, to relax and confuse them.

SOON, the victim becomes dizzy, sleepy and completely helpless.

BURKE and Hare invite the victim to lie down and rest a while.

WHILE THE VICTIM is fast asleep, they creep up and kill them!

Handy hint

Stay on your guard! Even though Burke and Hare are in prison, there are plenty more body snatchers still at work.

Zzzzzz

How many?

ood to see you again! You're not looking so well! I can see that the body snatcher murders have shocked you – as they have the rest of us!

Both Burke and Hare claim to be innocent, and accuse each other of the crimes. A date has been set for their trial – all Edinburgh thinks they are guilty.

Some of the victims

An English traveller, far from home.

A stranger from Glasgow.

A woman arrested for being drunk. Burke volunteered to look after her.

Mary Paterson, a pretty young runaway.

Joseph the Miller; he was old, sick and feeble.

A very old woman, who came to drink with Burke and Hare.

Her 12-year-old grandson, who was deaf.

An Edinburgh beggar woman, cold, half-starving.

No-one knows how many people Burke and Hare have killed. Some say 16, some say 17, some say 30! It seems that all their victims were strangers, outcasts, homeless, weak or helpless. Most had no family or friends to protect them. Isn't that tragic?

Have you heard? Hare has confessed to the killings, in return for a royal pardon. Only Burke will stand trial – but Hare will still have to face the angry public!

Handy hint

Choose charity! The Burke and Hare murders have revealed how many poor people live in Edinburgh's Old Town.

Mrs Ostler, a poor, hard-working washerwoman.

A female friend of Burke's family – all alone in the city.

Mary Haldane, a poor old homeless woman.

Another female family friend from faraway Ireland.

Mary Haldane's daughter Peggy, who asked after her mother at Burke's house.

Mary Docherty, a poor young woman.

Innocent victims

LONDON, 1831: Body snatchers Bishop and Williams also choose the poor and homeless as their victims. But when they take a well-known homeless child, nicknamed 'the Italian Boy', people notice. He is reported missing, and Bishop and Williams are both arrested.

Justice is done

In December 1828, Burke is tried for multiple murders, and found guilty. He is hanged in January 1829, in Edinburgh High Street.

A crowd of 25,000 gather to watch, all shouting abuse.

Before Burke's trial, most doctors, scientists and artists probably hadn't stopped to think where the bodies they used had come from. Now they have been forced to face an unpleasant truth: our recent medical and scientific progress has relied on a miserable trade.

> Hing the murtherar!
> (Hang the murderer!)

> Boo!

> I heard Hare got off scot free!

> I used to be in the medical profession, you know.

HELEN BURKE has been freed, but remains under suspicion. The court said her crime was 'not proven'. She's escaped from her lodgings, dodged angry crowds and is on a ship to Australia!

WILLIAM HARE is released from prison in 1829. He has also been attacked, and was badly injured. He was last seen begging in Carlisle, England. They say he's heading for London.

MARGARET HARE is going back to Ireland, chased by angry citizens. She's off to Glasgow to catch the first steamship she can. In Ireland, she'll be homeless and a beggar.

EDINBURGH CHILDREN have a new song:

"Up the close and down the stair..."

"...In the house with Burke and Hare..."

"...Burke's the butcher, Hare's the thief..."

"...Knox the man who buys the beef!"

Handy hint
Don't hang around with body snatchers! Even in Australia, Helen Burke's links with body snatchers will make her hated and feared. She'll die when her house burns down.

DR KNOX. There have been riots outside his Edinburgh house, and students stay away from his classes. Eventually he moves to London to work at the new cancer hospital there.

FITTING END? After the hanging, Burke's naked body is put on public display in Edinburgh – sixty people per minute walk past to see it. Then it is dissected, and the skeleton put on display in the Edinburgh University Medical School. (It's still there today.)

27

Good from evil
London, 1832

Amazingly – and encouragingly – good has come from the terrible story of Burke and Hare's murders. Now, three years after Burke was hanged, the British government has decided to pass a new law: the Anatomy Act. It will permit the dissection of any dead bodies that are not claimed by relatives.

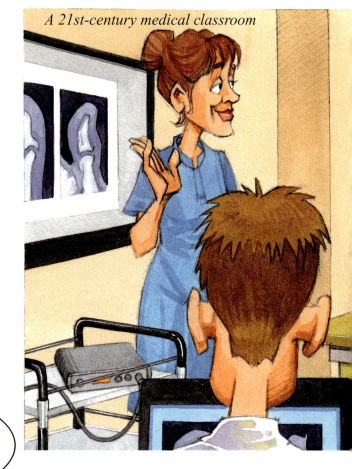

A 21st-century medical classroom

In the British Parliament, London:

Vote for science!
Vote for knowledge!

The new law means that there will be a steady, official, legal supply of bodies from workhouses (homes for the poor) and charity hospitals. Already the price of stolen bodies is falling, and body snatchers are going out of business. Now doctors, scientists and artists can study, learn and help humanity – without committing any crimes!

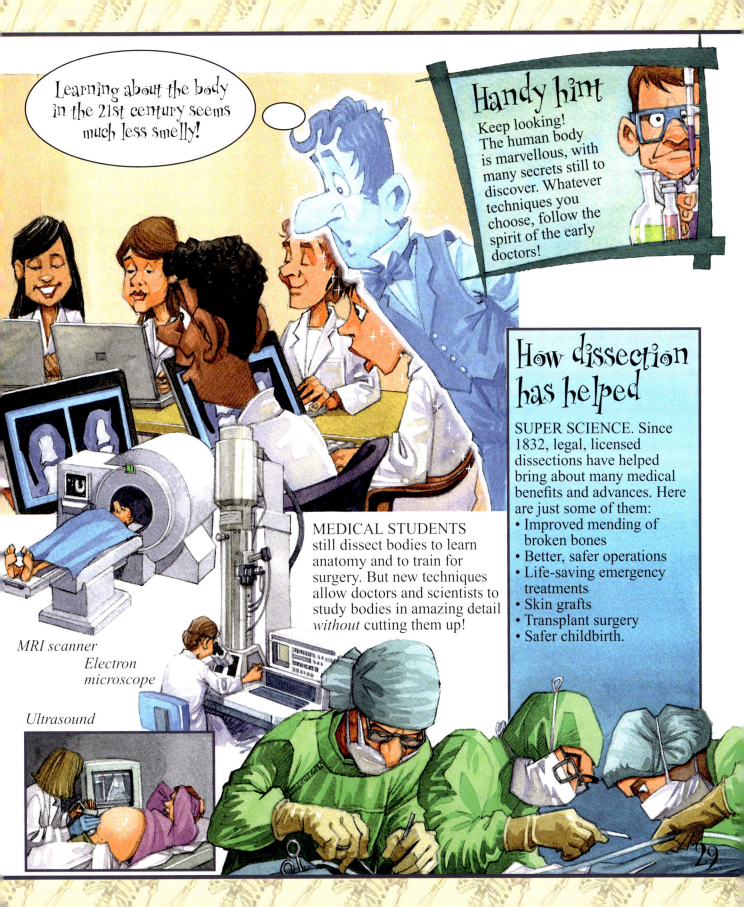

Learning about the body in the 21st century seems much less smelly!

Handy hint

Keep looking! The human body is marvellous, with many secrets still to discover. Whatever techniques you choose, follow the spirit of the early doctors!

How dissection has helped

SUPER SCIENCE. Since 1832, legal, licensed dissections have helped bring about many medical benefits and advances. Here are just some of them:
- Improved mending of broken bones
- Better, safer operations
- Life-saving emergency treatments
- Skin grafts
- Transplant surgery
- Safer childbirth.

MEDICAL STUDENTS still dissect bodies to learn anatomy and to train for surgery. But new techniques allow doctors and scientists to study bodies in amazing detail *without* cutting them up!

MRI scanner

Electron microscope

Ultrasound

29

Your guide to body snatching:

Step One:

Find a recently buried grave. Be sure to check for guardsman or grieving family members before getting to work, otherwise you too may soon be underground.

Step Two:

Get to work. Try not to spread the soil everywhere, otherwise it'll be very obvious that you have visited the grave. Using a wooden spade or shovel will be quieter than a metal one – the trick is not to get caught. Shhh!

Step Three:

After you have dug the hole, prepare to remove the body. Use a crowbar or similar tool to open the coffin; make sure you open it enough to remove the body. Drag the body out using rope. If someone checks, the coffin will still be in the grave. Don't pull too hard – a decapitated body will make you less money!

Step Four:

Strip the body! You aren't a thief, so you shouldn't steal the clothes that the body is wearing or any jewellery in the coffin. Throw any extra items you find back down the hole.

Step Five:

Disguise the body! You can't walk out of the cemetery with more people than when you arrived. A lot of body snatchers put the bodies in sacks as they are easier to carry and disguise.

Step Six:

Leave the grave as you found it. Making sure the grave looks the same as it did before you started is important, otherwise everyone will know that a body has been snatched.

Now you know how to do my job!

31

Timeline

4th September 1791

Robert Knox is born.

1826

Knox becomes head
of the anatomy school
in Edinburgh.

December 1827

Hare's tenant dies.
Burke and Hare sell
the body to Knox.

1792

William Burke and
William Hare are
born in Ireland.

1827

Burke moves into
Hare's lodging house
in Edinburgh.

January 1828–October 1828

The pair kill an estimated
16 victims, although it
could be as many as 30.

EDINBURGH

31st October 1828

The final victim, Margery Docherty (or Campbell), is killed. Hare is given a royal pardon after confessing to the murders.

February 1829

Hare is released from prison.

24th December 1828

Burke is tried for multiple murders.

28th January 1829

Burke is executed by hanging in Edinburgh High Street.

1832

The Anatomy Act is passed by the British government.

Did you know?

Knox was never tried for his involvement or association with the Burke and Hare murders, but in the end his career was ruined. He never asked where the bodies came from, which nearly led to his students catching him out when they recognised one of the bodies that they were due to dissect.

One of the victims, named James Wilson, was a recognisable figure on the streets of Edinburgh due to his disabilities. Students in Knox's class began to ask questions so Knox had to quickly remove his head and feet to avoid people realising that it was in fact the missing man.

Body snatching didn't just take place in Edinburgh. It was happening up and down the country for many years. One recorded incident in 1823 involved a 'Simon Spade', who quickly stopped body snatching after he accidentally dug up the body of his recently-deceased wife!

Operating at a similar time to Burke and Hare, four men named Bishop, Williams, Shields and May were later known as the 'London Burkers', after modelling their work on the Scottish body snatchers.

John Bishop and Thomas Williams were thought to be the leaders and after roughly 10 years of selling bodies, they were caught and sentenced to death for murder in 1831. The pair were caught out when trying to sell the body of a 14-year-old, nicknamed the 'Italian Boy', after the anatomist realised that the body had never been buried in the ground.

It was later discovered that Bishop and Williams had drowned the boy in a well. At the trial, Bishop confessed to selling roughly 1,000 bodies. Police never discovered how many were taken from graves and how many were murdered. Shields and May were saved by their fellow body snatchers after Bishop and Williams confessed to murder. In December 1831, the pair were hanged in front of a crowd of thirty-thousand people at Newgate Prison; their bodies were later given to medical schools for anatomy class dissection.

Other 19th-century murderers

Jack the Ripper

The most famous serial killer of all time stalked the streets of Whitechapel in London in 1888, killing at least five women. The killer was never caught, although many suspects have been identified over the years since. The gruesome murders caught the public's imagination at the time and were given extensive coverage by the press. The real events have inspired many stories and films.

Catherine Wilson

Whilst working as a nurse, Wilson would encourage her patients to leave money to her in their wills before poisoning them. She was only found guilty of one murder, but was believed at the time to have committed at least six more. She was executed in 1862, becoming the last woman to be hanged in public in London.

Herman Webster Mudgett

Mudgett is infamous for having designed a building that became known as the 'Murder Castle' where he tortured and killed visitors to the 1893 World's Columbian Exposition in Chicago. After killing his victims, Mudgett would try to cash their life insurance. After he was caught, he confessed to 27 murders, including one of his accomplices, but the police believed that he may have murdered many more. He was hanged in 1896.

Glossary

Anatomy The branch of science that deals with the structure of the body, including bone and muscle structure, and how the major organs work.

Anatomy Act A law passed by the British Parliament in 1832, that allowed any unclaimed dead bodies to be used for medical dissection.

Barber-surgeon A general doctor who treated the sick with minor operations and herbal medicine. The name comes from medieval times, when a surgeon also performed the role of barber.

Deceased (noun) A dead person.

Dissection Cutting up a body to study what is inside.

Electron microscope A type of microscope that uses electrons (parts of atoms) to enlarge an image.

Lecture An educational speech, used to teach large groups of students.

Lodger A person who pays money to live in part of someone else's house.

MRI (Magnetic Resonance Imaging) scanner A piece of medical equipment, used to see inside the body without cutting it open.

Not proven A verdict in Scottish law which means that there is not enough evidence to find the accused person guilty or not guilty.

Parliament In Great Britain, the place where laws are made.

Physician A medical doctor.

Resurrectionist A nickname for a body snatcher.

Royal pardon The forgiving of a crime, sometimes in return for giving important information about another criminal. A criminal who receives a royal pardon is not punished.

Silhouette A picture that shows only a solid black shape, like a shadow. Silhouettes were a popular form of art in the 19th century.

Glossary continued

Smallpox An infectious disease, unique to humans, that can cause death. It was one of the first diseases to be prevented using vaccination.

Specimen An example of a living thing, or part of a living thing, used for scientific study.

Transplant surgery A life-saving operation that replaces an unhealthy organ or body part with a healthy one from another person.

Ultrasound Technology that uses high-frequency sound waves to produce images. It can be used to see an unborn baby inside its mother.

Vaccination The use of a vaccine to prevent disease. A vaccine is a weakened form of a disease, given to a patient to help the body protect itself against a more serious form of the same disease.

Workhouse A place where poor people were given food and housing in return for doing work.

Index

For all the stuff you'd rather not know!

You will find loads of free stuff at: youwouldntwantto.be

Four free interactive web books

Free teachers' notes and activity sheets

12 free plays

You can book a play to be performed by Mr Dilly...

... and we hear he's top notch!

Send a free You Wouldn't Want to Be e-Postcard with 40 to choose from